Poophemisms
Over 1737 Fun Ways To Talk About Taking A Poop

Douglas Fir

DEDICATION

This book is dedicated to the CEO of Taco Bell, and the inventor of Metameucil. With loving dedication also to the plumbing industry, which has unstuck many a horrible situation for me over the years. And to my lovely dog brownie, who never forgets to leave a Tootsie Roll surprise on the neighbor's lawn.

CONTENTS

ACKNOWLEDGMENTS

As the author of this tome on feces, I would like to acknowledge myself for putting pen to paper. Also some people who work for me whose names I can't be bothered to learn. Further thanks for the bran muffins go to my Grannie, who always has my colon in mind.

1. #-A

12 Monkeys
movie title which could be a poophemism

21 gun salute

9 to 5
movie title which could be a poophemism

A Boy Named Charlie Brown
movie title which could be a poophemism

A Floating Crap Game

A Hard Day's Night
movie title which could be a poophemism

A Mighty Wind
movie title which could be a poophemism

A Nightmare on Elm Street
movie title which could be a poophemism

A Raisin in the Sun
movie title which could be a poophemism

A River Runs Through It
movie title which could be a poophemism

A rumble in the Bronx

A Series of Unfortunate Events
movie title which could be a poophemism

A sewer snake to release

A Time to Kill
movie title which could be a poophemism

A Trip to Bountiful
movie title which could be a poophemism

Abort a baby

Abuse the plumbing

Accept a dare

Accident

Add a wing to the manor

Add fabric softener

Add some pollution

Adjust the antenna

Adjust the shower head

Agent Brown

Air out the anus

Air out the ass

All the President's Men
movie title which could be a poophemism

AM BM

American Beauty
movie title which could be a poophemism

Anaconda action

Anal evisceration

Anal puke

Anal non-retentus

Analyze a log dump

Answer a call

Answer nature's call

Answer the call of the wild

Apocalypse Now
movie title which could be a poophemism

Apologize to my ex-wife

Apologize to the asshole

Arc one out

Army of Darkness
movie title which could be a poophemism

Arrange the furniture, move the stools

Arse biscuit

Arsefire

As Good As It Gets
movie title which could be a poophemism

Ass butter

Ass explosion

Ass of the Mohicans
movie title which could be a poophemism

Ass sneeze

Ass Volcano

Ass Vomit

Assemble a new product

Assquake

Attempt a top kill

Audit Your ASSets

August Rush
movie title which could be a poophemism

Awk one's pants

Aztec two-step

2. B

B.M.

Bab

Back one out

Back out the brown volvo

Back the big brown caddy out of the garage

Back the big brown motorhome out of the garage

Back The Bus Out Of The Garage

Back the trailer in

Backdraft
movie title which could be a poophemism

Ba-doop

Baffle NASA

Bait a trap

Bajsa

Bake A Hot Icicle

Bake a loaf

Bake a potato

Bake a russet

Bake brownies

Bakin' A Cake

Balance The Budget

Baptise Carl Malone

Baptise some larvae

Baptize my Baby Ruth

Baptize the school-kids

Barbarians at the gate

Battlefield Earth
movie title which could be a poophemism

Bear Movement
movie title which could be a poophemism

Bear down on a brown banshee

Beat Street
movie title which could be a poophemism

Become one with the animal kingdom

Become the porcelain assassin

Beeriod

Ben-Hur
movie title which could be a poophemism

Best in Show / Spinal Tap
movie title which could be a poophemism

Beyond Thunderdome
movie title which could be a poophemism

Big brown man knocking on the back door

Big Daddy
movie title which could be a poophemism

Big Fish
movie title which could be a poophemism

Big hit

Big jobby

Big one

bigjobs

Bill and Ted's Excellent Adventure
movie title which could be a poophemism

Bio Break

Biodome
movie title which could be a poophemism

Birth a brown bear

Birth a turd

Bite a train

Black Beauty
movie title which could be a poophemism

Black Hawk Down
movie title which could be a poophemism

Black Swan
movie title which could be a poophemism

Blast a dookie

Blast the pinworm cannon

Blazing Saddles
movie title which could be a poophemism

Blink

Blood Alley
movie title which could be a poophemism

Blood and Chocolate
movie title which could be a poophemism

Blood Diamonds
movie title which could be a poophemism

Bloop

Bloop-Bloop

Blow a butt plug

Blow an assload

Blow Mud

Blow one out

Blow The Butt Trumpet

Blow the load

Blow the tubes

Blow Up Heroshima

BM

Board the bus to Strong Anus City

Bob for apples

Body wax

Bog

Boggy

Bolt
accidental act of defecation.

Bomb dump

Bomb the Bowl

Bomb the oval office

Bomb the porcelain sea

Bomb The Tidy Bowl Man

Bomb the Tidy-bowl man

Bondi cigar

Boo-Boo

Boom Boom

Boom Town
movie title which could be a poophemism

booty hole burnout

Bootycakes

Booze poos

Boulder

Breach
movie title which could be a poophemism

Break off a dirty piece of spine

Break off a piece

Breakin 2 Electric Bugaloo
movie title which could be a poophemism

Breathless
movie title which could be a poophemism

Brew hot chocolate

Bring out endangered species

Brown balls

Brown bear coming out of his cave

Brown birds

Brown bobbin' ball

Brown bomb

Brown draGons

Brown Girl In The Ring

Brown hotdog

Brown remnants

Brown the bend

Brown trout

Brownhawk Down

Brownian Movement
movie title which could be a poophemism

Brownie batter

Brownie mix

Brownies

Browse the inventory

Build a bench

Build a better tomorrow

Build a dookie castle

Build a Gomer Pyle

Build a home for a dung beetle

Build a log cabin

Build A Poo Cabin

Bum brownie

Bum nuggets

Bung drop

Bunghole train has left the station

Bunny balls

Bunt

Burn a mule

Burn After Reading
movie title which could be a poophemism

Burn an old tire

Burn the midnight snack

Burners

Bury a quaker

Bury an elf

Bury cable

Bush is knocking at Cheney's door
having to take a poop, from the politicians

Business

Bust a crumpy

Bust a dook

Bust a grumpy

Bust a shit

Bust ass

Bust out a nug nug

Bust the o-ring

Butt butter

Butt clusters

Butt cobras

Butt gherkin

Butt gnome

Butt nugget

Butt nugget turdies

Butt nut

Butt-barf

Button

Buttsplosion

3 C

Caca

Cack

Call

Call of nature

Call one's uncle

Call the Governor

Cannonball Run
movie title which could be a poophemism

Canoodle with the fishes

Carbuncles

Carpet-bomb Afghanistan

Carpet bombing

Castaway
movie title which could be a poophemism

Catch a pooch

Catch Me If You Can
movie title which could be a poophemism

Catch up on some reading

Cause A Collision

Chalk the bowl

Change the channel

Change the oil

Charlie wants out of the chocolate factory

Charm an upside down brown snake

Chase out a chocolate monster

Check my messages

Check on yesterday's dinner

Check the evacuation route

Check the fuel reserves

Check The Pipes

Chevron moment

Chicken pecking out of one's butt
having to poop so badly that the poop is starting to poke out of the anus

Children of Men
movie title which could be a poophemism

Children of the Corn
movie title which could be a poophemism

Chitty Chitty Bang Bang
movie title which could be a poophemism

Chocolát
movie title which could be a poophemism

Chocolate banana

Chocolate bread loaf

Chocolate channel chewie

Chocolate exit

Chocolate factory of doom

Chocolate rain

Chocolate splat

Chocolate surprise

Chocolate syrup explosion

Chocolate time!

Choke A Brownie

Choke a darkie

Choke a loaf

Chop a log

Chop Some Butt Wood

Christen a boat

Christen the comfort station

Chuck the football

Chum for sewer rats
particularly for bloody diarrhea

Church van field trip

Clash of the Titans
movie title which could be a poophemism

Clean one's colon

Clean out the small intestine

Clean Out The Vertical File

Clean the ball pit

Clean the bathtub

Clean the chimney

Clean the fish tank

Clean the gutters

Clean the tuba

Cleanse the colon

Cleanse your sins

 Clear and Present Danger
movie title which could be a poophemism

Clear my throat

Clear Out Some Inventory

Clear the air

Clear The Hallways

Clear traffic on the Hershey Highway

Clear your head

Clearcut a cedar forest

Clip a biscuit

Clip off a cigar

Clone some turds

Close Encounters of the Third Kind
movie title which could be a poophemism

Cocken

Code 3

Coil a steamer

Coil a steamy

Coil one

Coil some rope
code used in medical situations to indicate that the patient has defecated

Coil the cobra

Colon Bowlin'

Colon Bowlin'

Come out Mr. Hankey

Coming to America
movie title which could be a poophemism

Commit yourself to the dumpatorium

Commune With Nature

Complete the download

Compose a waltz

Compound your interest

Conduct a movement

Conduct an important business transaction

Consider my options

Construct a new temple

Consult one's asstrological chart

Contaminate the dog dish

Contaminate the water

Contemplate my existence

Contribute to climate change.

Contribute to nature

Convert to metric

Cook a brown carrot

Cook a brown kielbasa

Cook a butt burrito

Cook a meatloaf in the porcelain saucepan

Cook some beans

Cook some chocolate

Cook some fudge

Cook some sausage

Cook up a pot of anal stew

Cool Hand Luke
movie title which could be a poophemism

Cool Runnings
movie title which could be a poophemism

Cop a shit

Cop a squat

Coprogenesis

Coronate Gluteus Maximus III

Coyote Ugly
movie title which could be a poophemism

Crack off a couple of bricks

Crack the dam on the rectum river

Crack the porcelain

Crank an eightball

Crap

Crap attack

Crap factory

Crap on deck that could choke a donkey

Create a custom extrusion

Create an ex-wife/ex-husband

Creature from the Black LaGoon
movie title which could be a poophemism

Crimp off a length

Crimson Tide
movie title which could be a poophemism

Cripp a crapple

Crocodile Dundee
movie title which could be a poophemism

Cross examine the witness

Crouching Tiger, Hidden DraGon
movie title which could be a poophemism

Crown

Crunch

Crunch one

Curl a hoot
to continually defecate

Curl One Down

Curl one off

Curl some pipe

Cut A Cable

Cut a promo

Cut against the grain

Cut and thread pipe

Cut off a load

Cut pipe

Cut rope

Cut some weight

Cut the line for the log flume

Cut the profit margin

Cut timber

Cut twine

4. D

Daily ritual

Damage the doulten

Dance with Duece Bigalog

Dangerous Liasons
movie title which could be a poophemism

Dark Star
movie title which could be a poophemism

Dark Victory
movie title which could be a poophemism

Das Boot
movie title which could be a poophemism

Deal funk

Debulk

Deceiver of Farts

De-cork the borking

De-corking the borking

De-do-do

Deep 6 a brownie

Deep Impact
movie title which could be a poophemism

Defend my client

Defile the porcelain throne

Defragment the hard drive

Deliver a wild pitch

Della Reese

Demolition Man
movie title which could be a poophemism

Deploy the little brown soldiers

Deport the Mexicans south of the border

Deprecate one's food

desecrate the throne room

Destroy the world

Detonate the dirty bomb

Deuce

Deuce Bigalow
movie title which could be a poophemism

Dig in the cat box

Dirtsnake

Dirty birth

Dirty Dancing
movie title which could be a poophemism

Dirty deeds

Dirty Harry
movie title which could be a poophemism

Dirty one's diaper

Dirty squirties

Discharge a prisoner

Discharge a waste
British euphemism for bowel movements

Discover lost coinage

Disembowel

Disemfiber

Dish out justice

Dispatch a Yankee

Dispense some soft-serve

Dispose of hazardous waste

Disrespect the toilet

Distill propane

Dive bomb

Divorce your dinner

Do

Do a burger

Do a do-do

Do a dog

Do a poo

Do brown

Do business with John

Do one's business

Do one's daily duty

Do one's dirt

Do one's ease

Do poopsie

Do some paperwork

Do some spring cleaning

Do the ass dance

Do the backdoor trot

Do the deed

Do the doo

Do the Fecal Funk

Do the Royal Squat

Do yard work
from the fact that a healthy adult should excrete daily enough turd so that when it was laid out end to end it would measure 1 yard (3 feet)

Dog Logs

Dogs barking at the back door

Doing the loose poops dance

Dominate

Donnie Darko
movie title which could be a poophemism

Doodey

Doodie

Doodle

Doo-Doo

Dook

Dook it

Dookey shute

Dookie

Down and Out in Beverly Hills
movie title which could be a poophemism

Down the periscope

Down the proctoscope

Down to Earth

Download

Download 5MB

Download a brownload

Download a corrupt file

Download a shit torrent

Download some brownware

Dr. Benjamin Fartlin

Dr. Tran's Quiet Log Time
movie title which could be a poophemism

Draw mud

Dreck

Drill for mud bunnies

Drippy doo-doo

Driver eight

Drop

Drop a bean

Drop A Biggie Smalls

Drop A Billy

Drop A Biscuit In The Basket

Drop a bomb

Drop a brick

Drop a brown snake

Drop a brown trout
when camping in the winter

Drop a chocolate cobra

Drop a coil

Drop a Cornback Rattler

Drop a darkie

Drop a deuce

Drop a dook

Drop a dookie

Drop a double deuce

Drop a fat load

Drop a gurdoodle

Drop a hoopsnake

Drop a hot bomb

Drop a jolst

Drop a Lincoln Log

Drop a load

Drop a loaf

Drop a Nessie in the Loch

Drop a nuke

Drop a pant size

Drop a pork loin

Drop a Purtle

Drop A Scafuri

Drop a scone

Drop a spike

Drop a Stanley Steamer

Drop a steak

Drop a steaming hemp rope

Drop a stinky log

Drop a stool

Drop a turd

Drop a wad in the porcelain God

Drop a Washburn

Drop an atomic bomb

Drop anchor

Drop ass Goblins

Drop bass
as in bass clef in music.

Drop beans

Drop bombs on Hiroshima

Drop chocolate buoys

Drop chop

Drop Dead Gorgeous
movie title which could be a poophemism

Drop depth charges on the Ty-D-Bowl Man

Drop doo-doo depth charges

Drop dumpage

Drop loggy log

Drop logs

Drop musTURD gas

Drop off the kids

Drop one from the poop deck

Drop Science

Drop Smokies

Drop some bait

Drop some clay

Drop some friends off at the lake

Drop some friends off at the pool

Drop Some Mud

Drop the Browns off at the Super Bowl

Drop the chalupa
a reference to a commercial from Taco Bell

Drop the Cosbies

Drop the Dangle

Drop the fatman

Drop the kids off at the pool

Drop the Mexican Boll Weevil

Drop the nuggets into the deep fryer

Drop the weights

Drop trout

Drop turds in the toilet

Drop wax

Drop wolf bait

Drop your ordinance

Drop Zone

Drown the kittens

Duke

Duke it out

Dump

Dump a Couch

Dump a dead grandma

Dump a load

Dump a load of gravel

Dump a stump

Dump an organic depth charge

Dump dinner

Dump truck

Dump your guts

Duncan Hines (Dunkin' Hinds)

Dung

Dunk the host in the wine

D-up

Dust crops

5 E

Ease nature

Eat Pray Love
movie title which could be a poophemism

Eden Log
movie title which could be a poophemism

Eject a round brown disc

Eject Goose
from the movie Top Gun

Eliminate a brown monkey

Eliminate a fecal waste

Eliminate body wastes

Eliminate evidence

empty (one's) bowels

Empty my arse

Empty the manure spreader

Empty the pooh pouch

Empty the poop shoot

Empty your anus

End Product

Enemy at the Gates

Enjoy a meatball sandwich

Enter The DraGon
movie title which could be a poophemism

Enter The Void
movie title which could be a poophemism

Erect an effigy

Escape from Alcatraz
movie title which could be a poophemism

Establish a trust fund

Evacuate

Evacuate one's bowels

Evacuate the building

Evacuate the survivors

Evacuate your bowels

Event Horizon
movie title which could be a poophemism

Every Little Movement
movie title which could be a poophemism

Evict the tenants

Excercise the uncertainty principle

Excercise your stock options

Excrete body wastes

Excrete fecal matter

Exercise the great guns

Exercise the push-me pull-you

Exit only trail

Exonerate my bowels

Exorcise the demons

Expel

Expel the hamster

Experiment in modern art

Explore the watery cave

Explosive decompression

Expunge

Expunge excess data

Extract
movie title which could be a poophemism

Extrude a Tootsie Roll

6. F

Factor a polynomial

Falling Down
movie title which could be a poophemism

Fantastic Voyage
movie title which could be a poophemism

Fart in the ice machine

Fart with character

Fat Albert
movie title which could be a poophemism

Fat Man and Little Boy
movie title which could be a poophemism

Faxing a shit to the toilet machine

Fecal fatality

Fecolith

Feed the dog

Feed the dung beetles

Feed the Goldfish

Feed the hungry puppy

Feed the pets

Feed the refugees

Feed the seagulls

Feed the sewer gators

Feed the shrimp (they're scavengers)

Feed the teabaggers

Feed the toilet

Feed the water Gods

Feed the white monster

Fertilize the ferns

Fertilize the plants
refers to defecating outdoors and on the ground, such as while camping

Fertilize the porcelainium

Fight rent control

Fight the rat

Fight with turdzilla

File some papers

Fill my pants

Fill the bowl

Fill the peanut butter jar

Fill the pot

Fill the septic

Fill up the duGout

Finance an expedition

Finding Nemo
movie title which could be a poophemism

Finish your thesis

Fire away

Fire down below

Fire off a missile

Fire out a Quincy

Fire rear thrusters

Fire stink bullets

Fire the 16 pounder
a cannon reference

Fire the cannon

Fire up the feco-matic

Fire your food

First Blood
movie title which could be a poophemism

Flag down the anus vendor

Flaunt the Weasel Cake

Flex your cheeks

Fling out a plooker

Float a boat

Float a log

Float a trout

Float one for the Gipper

Floodgates

Floss

Fluid Movement
movie title which could be a poophemism

Flunk a dunk

Flush feces

Flush the warp engine

Flushed Away
movie title which could be a poophemism

Fly food

Fo shizzle

Fold the dirty laundry

Forage for dingleberries

Force the duck to quack

Forces of Nature
movie title which could be a poophemism

Forge your legacy

Free a bog crocodile

Free my chocolate hostages

Free the chickens from the coop

Free the chocolate starfish

Free the legless dog to sea

Free the slaves

Free the turtles

Free Willy
movie title which could be a poophemism

Freshen up

Fried Green Tomatoes
movie title which could be a poophemism

Frighten the neighbors

Frisbee a bun fudge

Frog a log

Fudge

Full Metal Jacket
movie title which could be a poophemism

Full moon over troubled waters

Fumigate the bathroom

Furnish the kids area

7. G

Gagas

Geronimo
movie title which could be a poophemism

Get a burning desire to sit on porcelain

Get a turtle

Get down and dirty

Get into deep doo-doo

Get rid of some lunch

Gigli
movie title which could be a poophemism

Give a burial at sea

Give Back That Corn

Give birth

Give birth to a Baby Ruth

Give birth to a beauty queen

Give birth to a brown baby

Give birth to a chocolate baby boy

Give birth to a draGon

Give birth to a food baby

Give birth to a healthy brown baby

Give birth to a politician

Give birth to a Republican

Give birth to a San Francisco love child

Give birth to a state trooper

Give birth to a VB programmer

Give birth to another Texan

Give birth to sewer bass

Give birth to submarines

Give birth to the black eel

Give birth to the Spineless Brownfish

Give of oneself

Give Thanks and Praise

Give the food back

Give the hemmies some breathing room

Give the neighbors some food for thought

Gleaming the Cube
movie title which could be a poophemism

Go

Go backwards

Go boom boom

Go brown town

Go caca

Go christen the Organic Titanic

Go clip a yam

Go cocky

Go fecen'

Go for a mocha blast

Go for a penguin

Go for a Picnic

Go for a ring-stinger

Go for a Tom Tit

Go grunt

Go into a board meeting

Go into labor

Go Jackson Pollock
After the artist's splatter paintings

Go maverick

Go number 2

Go phone Elvis

Go poo poo

Go poop

Go poo-poo

Go poopy

Go pop

Go potty

Go sit down

Go sit down

Go stinky

Go take a Dilly

Go talk to Doug

Go the Distance
movie title which could be a poophemism

Go to a very small room

Go to bog

Go to have a talk with Mr.Hanky
South Park reference

Go to meet Jim Davidson

Go to number two

Go to Pakistan

Go to pottery class

Go to room 100

Go to see one's aunt

Go to talk to your mother

Go to the "little inventor's room"

Go to the batcave

Go to the bathroom

Go to the can

Go to the Chamber Of Secrets

Go to the chic sale

Go to the cloakroom

Go to the dunnee

Go to the happy room

Go to the John

Go to the khazi

Go to the library

Go to the necessarium

Go to the necessary house

Go to the privy

Go to the restitorial

Go to the restroom

Go To The Thinking Room

Go to the toilet

Go to the two-holer

Go to the WC

Go upstairs And check

Go whack

Goldfinger
movie title which could be a poophemism

Gone in 60 Seconds
movie title which could be a poophemism

Gone With The Wind
movie title which could be a poophemism

Goodbye Mr. Chips
movie title which could be a poophemism

Get a ups delivery

Got to go change my rear tire

Got to go put one on the radar

Got to go put one on the radar

Got to squirt

Gotta go push brown

Graph x^2

Grease one's hair

Grease the bowl

Grease the punchbowl

Green Apple Splatters

Greet Mr. Hankey

Grind one out

Grind the beef

Grindhouse
movie title which could be a poophemism

Grogin

Gronk

Grosse Pointe Blank
movie title which could be a poophemism

Grow a monkey tail

Grow a tail

Gruff nuts

Grumpy

Grunt

Guess Who's Coming to Dinner?
movie title which could be a poophemism

Guess whose Taco Bell experience

8. H-I

Hack a loaf

Hang a rat

Hang a root

Hang fresh ornaments

Hang ten, or at least eight

Happy Gilmour
movie title which could be a poophemism

Hard hit

Hatch a new boss

Hatch a new superintendent

Haul ashes

Have a case of the green apple splatters

Have a clear out

Have a code brown

Have a Conference Call

Have a core dump

Have a Crap

Have a food baby

Have a Mud Baby

Have a pony

Have a shit

Have a solid fart

Have a strain

Have a tissue issue

Have a turtle head poke out

Have an issue.

Have one in the departure lounge

Have Some Alone Time

Have some fun

Have to sit

Having Communion with Nature

Heat
movie title which could be a poophemism

Heave a Havana

Heave a Hershey

Heave the Log
movie title which could be a poophemism

Heim

Help out Dunkin' Donuts

Helping The Groundhog Find His Shadow

Hersheys special

Hersheys squirts

Hersheys surprise

Hide an egg

Hindenburg

Hit a double

Hit paydirt

Hit the can

Honey

Honey dip

Honey, I blew up the kids!
movie title which could be a poophemism

Honk out a dirtsnake

Hook up to a CO2 line

Horton Hears a Pooh
movie title which could be a poophemism

Hot Rod
movie title which could be a poophemism

Hound doggin'

How to Lose a Guy in 10 Days
movie title which could be a poophemism

How to Train Your DraGon
movie title which could be a poophemism

Howl's Moving Castle
movie title which could be a poophemism

Hulk
movie title which could be a poophemism

Hungry Hungry Hippos

Hunt for chocolate moose

Hunt for subs

Hurl a dung

Hurl a turd

Hurt Locker
movie title which could be a poophemism

I Am Legend
movie title which could be a poophemism

I gotta brown snake playing peek-a-boo with my butt crack

I gotta heave ho

Igby Goes Down
movie title which could be a poophemism

Ignite A Rectal Rocket

Imitate the Play-Doh Fun Factory

Improper use of the bathtub

In repose

Inagurate Barack Obama to the White House

Inception
movie title which could be a poophemism

Incontinence of the ass

Indiana Jones and the Temple of Doom
movie title which could be a poophemism

Inglorious Bastards
movie title which could be a poophemism

Inserting a SEAL Team

Inside Man
movie title which could be a poophemism

Inspect the facilities

Install new firmware

Internal Affairs
movie title which could be a poophemism

Internally developing a project

Interrogate the prisoner

Intestinal action

Intolerable Cruelty
movie title which could be a poophemism

Introduce the toilet to the bald man with the cigar

Invent euphemisms

Invest in mutual funds

Iron Giant
movie title which could be a poophemism

Islands in the Stream
movie title which could be a poophemism

It Came from Uranus
movie title which could be a poophemism

It Came from Within
movie title which could be a poophemism

It Happened One Night
movie title which could be a poophemism

It's a Wonderful Life
movie title which could be a poophemism

iWorks

9 J-L

Jackie Brown
movie title which could be a poophemism

Jagged Edge
movie title which could be a poophemism

James and the Giant Peach
movie title which could be a poophemism

Jettison the alien

Jim crack

Job

Join a fraternity

Jump to hyperspace

Jumpers away

Jumpers in the door

Just One of the Guys
movie title which could be a poophemism

Kick-Ass
movie title which could be a poophemism

Kill a dead eagle

Kill a hooker

Kill the bathroom

Kill the shitter

King Richard the Third

Knit a brown sweater

Kramer vs Kramer
movie title which could be a poophemism

Kurt Bevacqua

Lady in the Water
movie title which could be a poophemism

Launch a Butt Shuttle

Launch a coiler

Launch a corn canoe

Launch a corn rocket

Launch a deep-sea diver

Launch a log

Launch a missle

Launch a scud

Launch a ship

Launch a stink rocket

Launch a sub

Launch an ass rocket

Launch the brown torpedo

Launch the DSRV

Launch the schooner

Laxation

Lay a brick

Lay a brown egg

Lay a brownie

Lay a cable

Lay a deuce

Lay a Dirt Snake

Lay a Hank

Lay a log

Lay a pipeline

Lay a turd

Lay an egg

Lay assphalt

Lay down some spicy brown

Lay hot snakes

Lay one off

Lay pipe

Lay some brown carpet

Lay some sledge

Lay some wolf bait

Lead the Browns to the Super Bowl

Learn the backstroke

Leave a clue

Leave a deposit

Leave a floater

Leave a shit

Legend of Sleepy Hollow
movie title which could be a poophemism

Legends of the Fall
movie title which could be a poophemism

Lengthen the spine

Let a brown snake out of the cave

Let go

Let loose

Let my people Go

Let out the pooch

Let the big brown bear outta hibernation

Let The Corn Out

Let the dogs loose

Let the dogs out

Let the firetrucks loose

Let the toilet know who's boss

Lethal Weapon
movie title which could be a poophemism

Liberate France

Lift tail

used commonly among members of the furry fandom

Liquid Bummer

Liquid Satan

Liquidate your assets

Little brown fish

Little Nicky
movie title which could be a poophemism

Load of pulpwood

Load the crapper

Load your pants

Loafin'

Lock out a SEAL Team

Lock, Stock and Two Smoking Barrels
movie title which could be a poophemism

Log

Log into the toilet and make a huge download

Log jam

Log Jammed
movie title which could be a poophemism

Log out

Loosen my load

Lord Whitebowl demands a sacrifice

Lose a farting contest

Lose some weight

Lose some weight the quick way

Lose ten pounds in one minute

Lost Boys
movie title which could be a poophemism

Lucy-place a Charlie Brown kick

Lump your sums

10. M

Make

Make a banoogie
referring to an unusually large defecation, often clogging the toilet

Make a bog sausage

Make a brown rainbow

Make a bumpy

Make a chocolate hamburger

Make a Cleveland steamer

Make a core dump

make a corn dog

Make a delivery

Make a delivery to American Standard

Make a deposit

Make a deposit at the porcelain bank

Make a deposit in the Drop box

Make a donation to the democratic party

Make a donation to the porcelain collection plate

Make A Donation To The Porcelain God

Make a doo-doo

Make A Food-Rollup

Make a house

Make a little junk

Make a loaf

Make a log entry

Make a Mayan temple

Make a map

Make a milk shake

Make a Minnesota hand warmer

Make a new supervisor

Make a pass

Make a peanut salad

Make a politician

Make a question mark

Make a speech on parliament hill

Make a stinkmonkey

Make a stinky

Make a tail

Make a witches hat

Make ah ah

Make an appointment with Dr. John

Make bears

Make berries

Make caca

Make change for a dollar

Make chili

Make chocolate soft-serve

Make doo doo

Make everything come out all right

Make fossil fuel for the future

Make Fudge

Make gravy

Make grumpy faces

Make grunt sculpture

Make logs (or a log)

Make modern art

Make more actors for Jersey Shore

Make mud

Make new breed

Make poo poo

Make poopie

Make room

Make room for dinner

Make room for lunch

Make Some Butt Coffee

Make some butt gravy

Make some extra special brownies

Make some fertilizer

Make some haggis

Make some Scott-nuggets

Make some skid mark

Make some troshared_user chili

Make the donuts

Make the people in the apartment below scream in agony

Make Tootsie Rolls

Make turd

Make void

Make warm chocolate

Make waves

Make weight before the fight

Make you a twin

Making the chocolate snake

Man On Fire
movie title which could be a poophemism

Man the deck

Manufacture a three-coil steamer

Mariah Carey's Glitter
movie title which could be a poophemism

mark my spot

Mary Poppins
movie title which could be a poophemism

Max Payne
movie title which could be a poophemism

Measure the depths of the water below

Meditate

Meet Joe Black
movie title which could be a poophemism

Melt The Paint

Memento
movie title which could be a poophemism

Menace II Society
movie title which could be a poophemism

Mickey Fritt

Microwave a dachsund

Midnight Express
movie title which could be a poophemism

Million Dollar Baby
movie title which could be a poophemism

Misfart

Misspell balogna

Mobilize the Troops

Mold an action figure

Monopoly

Monsturd

Montezuma's Revenge
traveller's diarrhoea

Moon the Tidy Bowl Man

Morning constitutional

Morning smile

Move the mail

Movement

Movers and Shakers
movie title which could be a poophemism

Mr. MaGoo
movie title which could be a poophemism

Mud butt fire storm

Mudfuddle

Murder a brown snake

Murder a cloud

Murder a mud bunny

Murder a shit

Murder Oscar Meyer

My band's about to have an EP release

My butt's crowning

My Left Foot
movie title which could be a poophemism

My Poop Is Playing Peek-A-Boo

Mystic River
movie title which could be a poophemism

11. N-Q

Nature's call

Negotiate the release of the chocolate hostages

Nestle's Splat

Never Let Me Go
movie title which could be a poophemism

Night soil

Night soil archaic

Niskayuna

No One Here Gets Out Alive
movie title which could be a poophemism

Notorious
movie title which could be a poophemism

Nugg Nugg

Number ones

Number two

Observe Passover

Off to feed the pigs

Offload some freight

Old Yeller
movie title which could be a poophemism

Oliver Twist
movie title which could be a poophemism

On Golden Pond
movie title which could be a poophemism

On the captains chair making the captains log

Open the gates of hell

Open up a can of soup

Open wide for chunky

Operation "Clean Sweep"

Operation Dumbo Drop

Our inheritance

Outsource

Overdraft the bank account

Overthrow the monarchy

Pack a bowl

Pack your underwear

Paint the bowl

Paint the fence

Paint with the brown stuff
especially for a really wet one

Pap

Paradise Canyon
movie title which could be a poophemism

Park a custard

Park a load

Park some bark

Park your breakfast

Park your supper

Pass a load of coal down the chute

Pass the ass bass

Pass the baton

Pave the Hershey highway

Pay a visit to the old soldier's home

Pay homage to Burger King

Pay it Forward
movie title which could be a poophemism

Pay one's doctor bill

Pay reparations

Pay the band

Pay the plumber

Payback
movie title which could be a poophemism

Pearl Harbor

Pebbledash the bowl

Pebble-dash the porcelain

Pee butt

Pee out the wrong end

Peel the paint

Peel the wallpaper

Pennies from Heaven
movie title which could be a poophemism

People who like sausages shouldn't see how they're made!

Percolate butt coffee

Perform a junk shot

Phenomenon
movie title which could be a poophemism

Piledriver

Pinch (off) a loaf

Pinch a chimp

Pinch a crusty roll

Pinch a grumpy

Pinch a stink pickle

Pinch a yam

Pinch one off

Pinch-hitting for Kurt Bevacqua
a reference to the old brown uniforms worn in the 1970's and 1980's by the San DieGo Padres

Piss backwards

Piss rusty water out of your ass

Pitch a log

Plant a pine

Plant a steaming bouquet of brown roses

Plant brownies

Plant potatoes

Plant some corn

Plant strawberries

Play at the Toilet Bowl

Play bombs over Tokyo.

Play Craps

Play Kerplunk
Based on a kid's game

Play spin the turd

Play Stink-Jenga
From the kid's game

Play sudoku

Play the role of King Poo-Poo-A on his throne

Play the sandbox

Play with Mr. Hanky

Playing a small percussion instrument

Ploink

Plop

plop a load

Plop, plop, fizz, fizz, oh what a relief it is!

Plunk

Pocket Ninjas
movie title which could be a poophemism

Pohen

Poke the turtle's head out

Pollute the pond

Poo poo train

Pooh pooh

Poop

Poop a loop

Poop Deck Pirate
movie title which could be a poophemism

Poop soup

Poopie

Poopy doo

Poopy time

Poot

Pop a gooey

Pop a smurf

Pop a squat

Post to my blog

Pour out before the throne

Powder their noses

Practice Tetris

Prairie dog

Prance the fancy dishes

Pray to buddha

Pray to Sterculius
the Roman God of manure

Preach to the heathens

Press a loaf

Press an Avril Lavigne CD

Press coil

Print a retraction

Procrastinate backwards

Produce a brown baby

Produce some output

Produce the Glen Beck Show

Program the VCR

Prosecute the suspect

Provoke the gods

Puddin factory

Pull a few cones

Pull into defecation station

Pump a clump of dump out of my rump

Pump out the gutpaste

Punch a dook

Punch a growler

Punch a grumpy

Punch out a nugget

Punch out a steamer

Punish the porcelain

Punish the toilet

Purchase Louisiana from the French

Purge the database

Purp

Push a new build

Push brown
to need to defecate so badly that the feces is coming out a bit

Push fabric

Push out a grumpy

Push Some Putty

Put dents in the bowl

Put food in the dog's water

Put fruit in the bowl

Put In My Two Weeks Notice

Put My Knuckles To The Ground

Put My Thoughts Down On Paper

Put on brown lipstick

Put some work in at the factory

Put the bakery out of business

Put up a stink

Putting one through the hoop

Quake the porcelain

Quality me time

Quantum of Solace
movie title which could be a poophemism

Question traditional Christian values

Quick loading

Quicken the cleansing

12. R

Race up Bald Mountain

Raiders of the Lost Ark
movie title which could be a poophemism

Ran
movie title which could be a poophemism

Rapid Weight Loss Center

Read A Book

Read the minutes from the last meeting

Read the New Yorker

Reagan's revenge

Really finish my breakfast

Rear Window
movie title which could be a poophemism

Recaulk the shitter

Receive a summons

Recompile the source code

Recreate Hurricane Katrina

Recycle fiber

Recycle my last meal

Recycle some cellulose

Red light flashing

Redecorate the bathroom

Re-enact The Dam Busters

Refill Palin's brain
from the political candidate

Refill the bowl with chili

Refill the ice cube tray

Refinance the mortgage

Reflect on past descisions

Refresh the body

Reign of Fire
movie title which could be a poophemism

Release a depth charge

Release a dung bomb

Release a sewer snake

Release a sewer trout

Release the beasts

Release the bombs

Release the chocolate hostages

Release the cotton-sniffing turtle into the porcelain pond

Release the demons

Release the hostages

Release the hounds

Release the Kraken

Release the prisoner

Release your payload

Relieve one's bowels

Relieve oneself

Remains of the Day
movie title which could be a poophemism

Remember The Titans
movie title which could be a poophemism

Remove a butt tampon

Replant corn

Reservoir Dogs
movie title which could be a poophemism

Resist the arrest

Re-stock the pond with brown trout

Reverse a Ho-Ho

Reverse-park your breakfast

Revisit my last meal

Revolve the beavers

Rid a solid waste

Ride a pony and trap

Ride the ceramic carthorse

Ride the hoop

Ride the porcelain bus

Ride the porcelain pony

Ride the porcelain tiger

Ride the porcelain truckRiding the Hershey Highway

Rig the election

Ring of fire

Ring the buoy

Ring the church bells

Rinse the flatware

Rip a duece

Risky Business
movie title which could be a poophemism

Rob the bakery

Rock your rectum

Rocky
movie title which could be a poophemism

Roll a ciger

Roll a log

Roll a Nut Log

Roll for half damage

Roll the oak barrel

Roll a cigar

Rendezvous with last night's supper

Rosemary's Baby
movie title which could be a poophemism

Rotate it the hard way

Rumbling Bowels

Run Bitch Run
movie title which could be a poophemism

Run Silent Run Deep
movie title which could be a poophemism

Run Silent, Run Deep
movie title which could be a poophemism

Running Man
movie title which could be a poophemism

Rush Hour
movie title which could be a poophemism

13. S

Sacrifice to the Toilet/Porcelain God

Salad shooter

Sandblast the toilet

Saturday morning special

Saw off a log

Say goodbye to Mr. Brown

Scare fish

Scare up a tater

Scat in the hat

Scatberg

Scatman

Scatter bombing

Scooby Doo
movie title which could be a poophemism

Search for hidden treasure

Secret activity #1

See a man about a dog

See a man about a horse

See off the bus full of colonels (kernels)

Seek revenge for the brown bomber

Send a care package

Send a fax

Send A Message To The White House

Send a part of you off to sea

Send a posse out after some river rats

Send another potential American Idol to Hollywood

Send Fidel a love letter

Send junk mail to my Spam folder

Send Some Cigars Back To Cuba

Send some sailors to sea

Send the U.S.S. Constipation on her maiden voyage

Serve Up A Poo Poo Platter

Seven Pounds
movie title which could be a poophemism

Sewer trout

Shaft
movie title which could be a poophemism

Shake a brown bomber

Shake a brown monkey

Shake a few clinkers out

Shake a tit

Shake one's grates

Shake the ashes out

Shake your booty

Shane
movie title which could be a poophemism

Shape the meatloaf

Shee-Shee

Shik

Ship a logs

Shit

Shit a flock of sparrows

Shit bricks
Houses or apartments as substitutes for higher quantity

Shitdown

Shit's on the way

Shit purple nickles

Shitty weight loss program

Shizzle in the tizzle

Shoo-shoo

Shoot

Shoot a dog

Shoot bunnies

Shoot out a sewer pickle

Shoot out a shoggoth
an H.P. Lovecraft reference

Shoot some craps

Shoot the hershey squirts
diarrhea

Shoot your meatloaf

Shooter
movie title which could be a poophemism

Shove out a stink pole

Shower the room with roses

Shrug off global warming

Shtounga

Shump

Sign a contract with the Browns

Silent Running
movie title which could be a poophemism

Sing a duet

Sing in a lower octave

Sing tenor through your anus

Sing with Michael Bolton

Sink a link

Sink a sausage

Sink battleships

Sink submarines

Sink the Bismark

Sit on my nest of chocolate eggs

Sit on the bowl

Sit on the can

sit on the crapper

Sit on the throne

Sit on the throne of porcelain

Skew the grading curve

Skip detention

Skita

Slam

Slap the pod

Slide one out

Slither
movie title which could be a poophemism

Slop gruel in Oliver's bowl

Sloppy jalopy

Slough the ace

Smash

Smear the bowl

Smell up the house

Smoke a brown dooby

Smokin' Aces
movie title which could be a poophemism

Snake Race

Snakes On A Plane
movie title which could be a poophemism

Snap a log

Snap a yambo

Snap into a Slim Jim

Snap one off

Snip off a length of dirty spine

Soil one's pants

Solid fart

Solve for x

Solve the energy crisis

Solve the natural logarithm for food

Some Like It Hot
movie title which could be a poophemism

Something Wicked This Way Comes
movie title which could be a poophemism

Spackle the porcelain

Sparkle

Spartacus
movie title which could be a poophemism

Spawn
movie title which could be a poophemism

Speak with the Arabs

Speech from the throne

Spend a penny

Spend quality time with the porcelain Buddha

Sphincter snot

Sphincter spew

Sphincter spurt

Spice up the sausage

spike a bird's nose

Spike a football

Spit mud

Splash mud

Splash pumpkins

Split some oak

Sploosh

Spray and wipe

Spray the crops

Spray-paint the porcelain

Spraypaint the toilet

Sprout a tail

Squash out a fun log

Squash out a yule log

Squat

Squat a grump

Squat and clench

Squat and push

Squat in a pot

Squeal
movie title which could be a poophemism

Squeeze a coily

Squeeze a fresh slurpy

Squeeze a Hershey's kiss

Squeeze a loaf

Squeeze a steamer

Squeeze off a few rounds

Squeeze one out

Squeeze out a fat one

Squeeze Out A Flesh Slurpee

Squeeze Out A Lincoln

Squeeze out those last few calories

Squeeze out those last few calories

Squeeze the butt mustard

Squeeze the cheese

Squeeze the salami

Squirt juice
diarrhea

Squitters

St. Elmo's Fire
movie title which could be a poophemism

Stain the porcelain

Stall a brown sedan

Start a poolitical rights movement

Steamer

Step into the office

Stick it to the man

Stinky doop

Stock the lake with brown trout

Stock the pond with some brown trout
especially for people who spend an excessive time in the bathroom
at work

Stoke the fire

Stool

Stool Pigeon
movie title which could be a poophemism

Stranglehold On A Darkie

Stream Nixie
naval expression referring to an anti-submarine device towed
behind a ship by a long, thick, possibly brown cable

Stretch a muscle

Stretch The Anus

Stretch the sphincter muscle

Stuck on You
movie title which could be a poophemism

Studies in Movement
movie title which could be a poophemism

Study at the Library

Study my toes

Study one's Process Design notes

Stuff a punch

Submit your résumé

Sudden Impact
movie title which could be a poophemism

Swim through a dollhouse

Swimming with Sharks
movie title which could be a poophemism

Swiss Movement
movie title which could be a poophemism

14. T

Taint the cloth

Take a "Schroeder"

Take a 20

Take a biological break

Take a brew

Take a chat

Take a Count Dooku
From the Star Wars series

Take a crap

Take a critical ambient to the lab

Take a crunch

Take a deuce

Take a digger

Take a digi

Take a doogie

Take a dookey from the ace

Take a dookie

Take a duke

Take a dump

Take a good one

Take a growler

Take a grump

Take a healthy

Take a leak out one's ass

Take a load off your mind

Take a long time to load

Take a lovely

Take a manly

Take a Nixon

Take a Pelosi and wipe my Biden
from the politicians
Take a plane crash

Take a plumper

Take a poo

Take a poop

Take a prestige class

Take a rest

Take a Rodney

Take a Shatner

Take a shit

Take a signal 92

Take a slam

Take a smash

Take a snap

Take a squat

Take a squish

Take a steamer

Take a Tarzan

Take a uni
Go to the bathroom in the woods.

Take a wiz

Take a Yok

Take an Irish shave

Take an SS CapolonGo

Take Care of Business
movie title which could be a poophemism

Take care of one's business

Take care of the three S's
Shit, shower and shave

Take my talents to south beach

Take Seal Team Six to the insertion point

Take the browns to the Astro Dome

Take the Browns to the Superbowl

Take the Cosby kids to the pool

Take the kids for a swim

Take the kids to the waterslide

Take the mains offline and eject the warp coil

Take the morning curl

Take the yacht out

Takers
movie title which could be a poophemism

Talk some shit to John

Talk to a man about a horse

Talk to a man about a mule

Tall In The Saddle
movie title which could be a poophemism

Tenspeed & Brownshoe
movie title which could be a poophemism

Test gravity

Test the plumbing

That Thing You Do
movie title which could be a poophemism

The Abyss
movie title which could be a poophemism

The Art of Movement
movie title which could be a poophemism

The Bends

The Big Lebowski
movie title which could be a poophemism

The Big Red One
movie title which could be a poophemism

The Black Hole
movie title which could be a poophemism

The Black Stallion
movie title which could be a poophemism

The Blind Side
movie title which could be a poophemism

The Blob
movie title which could be a poophemism

The Blue Lagoon
movie title which could be a poophemism

The bog monster cometh

The Bone Collector
movie title which could be a poophemism

The Bourne Supremacy
movie title which could be a poophemism

The Breakfast Club
movie title which could be a poophemism

The Bridge on the River Kwai
movie title which could be a poophemism

The Brown Crown

The Brown Derby
movie title which could be a poophemism

The brown dog scratches at the cotton fence

The chunky sputters

The Crying Game
movie title which could be a poophemism

The Dark Knight
movie title which could be a poophemism

The Dark Lurking
movie title which could be a poophemism

The Day the Earth Stood Still
movie title which could be a poophemism

The Deep
movie title which could be a poophemism

The Departed
movie title which could be a poophemism

The deuce is loose

The Dirty Dozen
movie title which could be a poophemism

The Fast and the Furious
movie title which could be a poophemism

The Fifth Element
movie title which could be a poophemism

The Forbidden Planet
movie title which could be a poophemism

The Force Behind Its Movement
movie title which could be a poophemism

The fudge factory is working overtime

The Gift
movie title which could be a poophemism

The Good, The Bad and the Ugly
movie title which could be a poophemism

The Graduate
movie title which could be a poophemism

The Grapes of Wrath
movie title which could be a poophemism

The Great Escape
movie title which could be a poophemism

The Great Movement
movie title which could be a poophemism

The Green Berets
movie title which could be a poophemism

The Green Mile
movie title which could be a poophemism

The green-apple quicksteps

The Hangover
movie title which could be a poophemism

The Howling
movie title which could be a poophemism

The Human Stain
movie title which could be a poophemism

The Hunt For Red October
movie title which could be a poophemism

The Incredible Mr. Limpet
movie title which could be a poophemism

The Italian Job
movie title which could be a poophemism

The Last Airbender
movie title which could be a poophemism

The Last Exorcism
movie title which could be a poophemism

The Last Starfighter
movie title which could be a poophemism

The Lion, the Witch, AND the Wardrobe
movie title which could be a poophemism

The Long Voyage
movie title which could be a poophemism

The Longest Day
movie title which could be a poophemism

The Lords of Dog Town
movie title which could be a poophemism

The malady

The Man Who Fell To Earth
movie title which could be a poophemism

The Matrix Reloaded
movie title which could be a poophemism

The Neverending Story
movie title which could be a poophemism

The Nightmare before Christmas
movie title which could be a poophemism

The Pelican Brief
movie title which could be a poophemism

The People Under the Stairs
movie title which could be a poophemism

The Phantom Menace
movie title which could be a poophemism

The Polar Express
movie title which could be a poophemism

The Postman Always Rings Twice
movie title which could be a poophemism

The Prestige
movie title which could be a poophemism

The Progressive Movement
movie title which could be a poophemism

The Return of the King
movie title which could be a poophemism

The Ring
movie title which could be a poophemism

The Rock
movie title which could be a poophemism

The Rocky Horror Picture Show
movie title which could be a poophemism

The Runs

The Sand Pebbles
movie title which could be a poophemism

The Seventh Seal
movie title which could be a poophemism

The Shawshank Redemption
movie title which could be a poophemism

The Shining
movie title which could be a poophemism

The Shootist
movie title which could be a poophemism

The Sting
movie title which could be a poophemism

The Sum of All Fears
movie title which could be a poophemism

The Thin Red Line
movie title which could be a poophemism

The Thing
movie title which could be a poophemism

The Three S's
shit, shower and shave

The Tingler
movie title which could be a poophemism

The Transporter
movie title which could be a poophemism

The turtle pops his head out

The Unbearable Lightness of Being
movie title which could be a poophemism

The Usual Suspects
movie title which could be a poophemism

The Wayward Cloud
movie title which could be a poophemism

The Women
movie title which could be a poophemism

The Wood
movie title which could be a poophemism

There Will Be Blood
movie title which could be a poophemism

Think of your Face

Think outside of the box

Think positively

Thirteen Days
movie title which could be a poophemism

Thora (Hird)
Rhyming slang on 'turd', Thora Hird, veteran British actress, died in 2003

Through the Ass Darkly
movie title which could be a poophemism (kind of)

Throw a chip

Throw a Curve Ball

Throw a load of old shoes out of a loft

Throw a pot

Throw a wild deuce in the pot

Throw down some brown

Throw in the towel

Throw off the cake

Throw the deuce

Throw up backwards

Thunderball
movie title which could be a poophemism

Tinkerbell and the Lost Treasure
movie title which could be a poophemism

Titanic
movie title which could be a poophemism

Tootsie

Torpedo Alley
movie title which could be a poophemism

Torpedo bays are now open

Torque a moon-fish

Torque a wicked cable

Touch cloth
To have to poop so badly that the poop itself is touching your underwear

Touch cotton
To have to poop so badly that the poop itself is touching your underwear

Train a pet to jump through the hoop

Trainspotting
movie title which could be a poophemism

Transanal meditation

Transparent Movement
movie title which could be a poophemism

Trash the hash

Tremors
movie title which could be a poophemism

Tropic Thunder
movie title which could be a poophemism

Trouser chili

Try Scottish cuisine

Tuesday Afternoons

Turd

Turd cutting

Turd tsunami

Turn down the thermostat

Turn my back on the ocean

Turn on the sausage maker

Turn the wienermobile into a submarine

Turnpike a poo

Turtle time

Twist out a nine coiler

Twister
movie title which could be a poophemism

15. U-Z

UH-OH!

Unbreakable
movie title which could be a poophemism

Un-brew coffee

Unchain a melody

Unclog the pipes

Uncork the bunghole

Unforgiven
movie title which could be a poophemism

Unhinge the doors

Unhitch a load

Unify classical physics with quantum mechanics

Unleash a load of fury

Unleash the brown draGon

Unleash the demons

Unleash the holy leviathan

Unleash the logs of war

Unlikely Traveler

Unload
Defecation, usually on vacation, when you defacate in your pants away from a toilet.

Unload a high brown

Unload the paypacket

Unload the trunk

Unloading a batch of cigars

Untie the balloon knot

Update my blog

Update the captain's log

Upgrade my Thetan Level

Upper decker

Upside-down hot fudge sundae

Use the save point

Utilize the poop shoot

Vacate

Vacate the premises

Vacate the premises

Vertigo
movie title which could be a poophemism

Viscous Biscuit

Visit Boston

Visit Fonzie's Office

Visit Fortress Of Solitude

Visit mother nature

Visit Mr. Hanky

Visit Mr. Limbaugh

Visit Mr. Stallman

Visit murphy closet

Visit Narnia

Visit the brown mound

Visit the chamber of commerce

Visit the chim

Visit the crapper

Visit the library

Visit the little girls' room

Visit the loo

Visit the Pope

Visit the sandbox

Visit the throne

Visit the toilet for a poo-poo

Visit Uncle Charley

Visit Uncle Grumpy

Void the bowels

Vote for president

Wag the Dog
movie title which could be a poophemism

Wait for the Movement

Waiting For Guffman
movie title which could be a poophemism

Wash the walls

Watch a dolphin splash

Watch reruns of the Cosbys

Watch the Jamaican bobsled team

Watership Down
movie title which could be a poophemism

Waterworld
movie title which could be a poophemism

Wear a hat

Weasel nosing

Weigh your alternatives

What Lies Beneath
movie title which could be a poophemism

Where even the emperor must go on foot

Where the Red Fern Grows
movie title which could be a poophemism

Where There's a Will There's a Way
movie title which could be a poophemism

William (Pitt)

William Shattner(ing)

Woke up Winnie The Pooh

Wolf bait

Work on a grunt sculpture

Work the scissor-bone

Wrestle a brown corn-belly snake

Wrestle a leprechaun

Wrestling a leprecon

Write about the global economy

Write an autobiography

Write in iambic pentameter

Write one's name with brown chalk

Xerox a copy of the bad stuff

Yank the worm out of the hole

Yell at Mrs. Johnson

Yell at the bathroom ceiling

Yellow alert

Yellow Submarine
movie title which could be a poophemism

Yodel in the canyon

Yucky

Zap the porcelain

ABOUT THE AUTHOR

Douglas "Uncle Dougie" Fir is the proud product of a public education who was born in a state which allows first cousins to marry. Dragging himself from abject poverty into inveterate unemployment, Uncle Dougie is one of the guys who puts down the words in the stellar web site – The Maine Gazette (mainegazette.com). Someday he'd like to travel the world and crap in a fountain near the Louvre.

Made in the USA
Lexington, KY
18 December 2014